Machine Learning for Beginners

A History, A Basic Outline, And The Moral
Quandary It Presents To Humankind

By Alec Gilliam

Table of Contents

What is Machine Learning?

Machine learning is the ability of artificial intelligence to learn and adapt without being explicitly programmed to perform a pre-prescribed outcome. It is a machine's ability to act on its own, to learn. Many forms of artificial intelligence use a wide variety of tactics to employ this, including pattern recognition and unsupervised learning algorithms. Currently, there is a lot of excitement and focus on machine learning in the world of programming, as it is often interpreted to imply a limitless future in artificial intelligence: a world in which machines could adapt and respond to a wide variety of stimuli and factors without direct programming response from a human. A world in which machines could learn and adapt on their own.

Often, machine learning is seen as the missing "human" element in machines; the ability for machines to start to fill the gap between what makes us human and what makes machines; a sense of responsiveness and flexibility in a given environment and a set of circumstances. By and large, the goal of learning is to be able to generalize: to take a set of lived circumstances, and to be able to extrapolate a sense of patterning about what the future holds, and how the person should respond to similar given situations. Machine learning is similar; it is the attempt to program machines so that they can generalize about future possibilities and probabilities based on data sets. In short- machine learning is the quest to get machines to think like humans. This takes a wide variety of forms and is used for a wide variety of purposes.

In the following pages, we will explore the history of machine learning, the academic and scientific elements that make up the study, as well as touching on this moral and philosophical space that they occupy.

The History of Machine Learning

The origins of machine learning are often traced back to 1950 when Alan Turing invented the "Turing Test", designed to test machines. To pass the test, a machine would need to respond closely enough to human responsiveness that it would fool a human. From this moment forward, scientists have tried to pass the test with various machines. Today, the Turing Test is still a benchmark that programmers strive for. What is that essential human element, and how can it be mechanically and artificially be reproduced?

In 1962 the first computer program was invented; a game of checkers that improved upon itself the more it was played, by adding new moves to its rapport taught to it by its human opponent. It was learning, in a sense, but based on mimicry. Through the 1950s and 60s, the first beginnings of artificial neural networks were invented by Frank Rosenblatt, a crucial step in machine learning. The artificial neural networks were based on the way that the human brain functioned- the biological neural network. In 1985, Terry Sejnowski created a program that learned to speak words modeled off of the way that a human baby learns. In the 1990s, with the invention and spread of the internet, scientists began to move from a knowledge-based approach for learning to a data-based approach; allowing their machines access to vast and varied forms of data. In a watershed moment, IBM's Deep Blue machine beat the world champion in a chess tournament, one of the first moments of a machine out-performing human ingenuity. In 2006, Geoffrey Hinton coined a term for the algorithms he was working with that allowed machines to "see" objects in a room or video and respond to them with human-like fluidity: he called it "deep learning", and it would become a conceptual way of thinking about data and machine learning that would change things forever. In 2006, technology emerged that allows machines to read human facial expressions and bodies as data, which allows humans to interact directly with machines.

In the following years, voice recognition, retina scanning, automated office assistants and highly personalized online experiences have become the norm. We are living more and more with the expectation of machines that can interact with us as if they were fellow humans. Our machines increasingly function to expand our knowledge and extend our bodies and minds into the various worlds we inhabit. Currently, there are prototypes of self-driving cars in Nevada, with stated goals of having them become a permanent part of our infrastructure across the country. There are prototypes for robot nannies and interactive interfaces for health care. More and more, the expectations of science fiction are being met: our machines have become almost life-like in so many ways. But as machines take on increasingly important roles in our world and cultural consciousness, including taking on jobs or serving roles that have always been held by humans, important and complex moral and philosophical questions start to emerge about what it means to be human, and what space a machine can inhabit in our world. We should both understand how this technology works, and also understand and address the moral questions that this kind of technology brings to light.

Examples of Machine Learning

One of the easiest ways to explore and understand machine learning is to start to see examples of it in our daily lives. When approaching the field of machine learning for the first time, its very easy to see it as a highly scientific field, separated out from our daily understanding. But in actuality, examples of machine learning exist all around us and populates our mundane daily lives, as well as our entertainment and dreams of the future. We already live in tandem with machines, and it seems as though the boundaries between human and machine will become more and more blurry as time goes on.

Machine learning is used in the way we search for things on the internet, the way targeting marketing works, our email systems, our libraries, hospitals, traffic systems, GPS, etc. We use machine learning in fraud detection software, online recommendation programs utilized by companies like Amazon and Netflix, and of course, the heavily-publicized self-driving Google car. Because machine learning is specifically targeted to work in tandem with human behavior, these systems are often made invisible to us, which illustrates their value and possibility in everyday life.

In the example of something like Amazon or Netflix, because the program is anticipating your needs and matching them, you are less likely to spend a lot of time marveling over it, and instead, just use it. It's modeled after our brains, so it makes sense because the program is largely an extension of the way the human mind thinks. You are likely sitting on Netflix musing to yourself "God, I really liked that movie last week about the basketball team. I wonder if there's another good movie about sports..." and in that exact moment, algorithms have already provided Netflix with the answer, built off of your past behavior, modeled after the way the human brain thinks and interacts with the world. The machine is filling a need-gap in your own behavior. Machine learning has become, in many cases, an extension of how your brain would work if it just had access to more information and more resources for sorting that information.

In the more extroverted examples, such as the self-driving cars from Google, it's enough of a jump forward from something that we are used to doing ourselves, that we are able to see the strides forward, and it is awe-inspiring and unnerving. In examples such as these, we can see what machine learning is capable of for humankind when it steps into larger situations: it is not just a question of how technology could step in and extend your brain's scope and reach for consumer or entertainment needs, it becomes the thrilling proposition of what artificial intelligence could do for us if it could also extend the ability of our large-scale transport systems, and of our bodies. If we allow ourselves to contemplate these things truly, the question becomes in essence; what is the possibility of artificial intelligence in every part of our cognitive and physical functioning? The answer to this is still unfolding, and it means that machine learning in artificial intelligence is not just a scientific or a programming question, but instead, it is also a social and a philosophical quandary. For machine learning to advance our societies, it is crucial that all these questions are answered, and evidenced in the ways that we use machine learning.

How Does Machine Learning Work?

Machine learning utilizes a wide variety of models and processes to teach a machine how to learn. At its core, what that means is that machines mine an existing data set for information, examples, and strings of actions that allows them to look at similar situations and make judgements about how to act, react, or interact with a new data set, from information from the internet to a physical environment, to the sound of a human voice or eye contact.

Many of the algorithms that make this kind of learning possible come from a branch of theoretical computer science known as computational learning theory. The main concepts and common approaches to machine learning are outlined below.

Common Approaches and Terms in Machine Learning

Theoretical Computer Science

Theoretical computer science is a subset of the larger field of computer science, which is largely concerned with mathematical principles of computing. Theoretical computer science regularly pulls from more abstract ideas and includes applied computational and coding theory. Even though it is a subset of computer science, theoretical computer science is not excluded from the world of basic mathematics and computer science, which it heavily pulls from. Often, theoretical computer science delves deep into the semiotics of computing and models of learning and knowledge assimilation. It is a field that asks people to think deeply about the models that we use for finding knowledge, storing it, and making it available and usable to ourselves, and it uses computers as a way to explore and expand what is possible about our relationship with information and data. Machine learning comes directly out of the field of theoretical computer science.

Computational Learning Theory/Association Rule Learning

One of the most basic ways that machine learning function is through computational learning theory. At its core, computational learning theory is a system that allows people to look at large amounts of data, and mine the sets for meaningful and interesting connections and results. The basic idea is very simple: in looking at large volumes of data, repeat existing collieries exist for a large logic. These patterns create "rules" which are used to draw meaningful assumptions. Perhaps a good example is looking at this technology in POS systems, the point of sale technology used in restaurants, stores, and supermarkets.

Let's say that a supermarket applies computational learning theory to their POS records. Let's say that they notice that if a person buys cereal, they almost always buy milk, and they often buy fruit as well. As a human being who is familiar with the abstract concept of "breakfast", this makes a lot of sense, and we know why these items are grouped together in a shopping cart. Somebody needs breakfast items! The supermarket would accommodate this information by making those items easily accessible near each other or clearly advertised in that section. The computation learning theory technology in your POS system can't tell you all the functional human needs that let you understand why those objects are grouped together, but it can tell you that they are grouped together. It might seem simple in this example, but if the data set becomes way bigger and/or more complex, you can easily see how this kind of data interpretation can be really useful in a wide variety of contexts.

In contrast to sequence mining, computational learning theory doesn't look at the order or sequence of things mixed together, just that they group together, and any resulting interesting connections are drawn from that cluster. Providing the information that allows us to ask the question "what exists together and why?" is an essential human function, and computational learning theory illustrates how when the data sets become too large for a single human brain to sort, order, and draw conclusions from, machine learning can step in.

This concept is widely utilized in technology for intrusion detection, web mining usage, market basket analysis, and many other functions.

Pattern Recognition

Pattern recognition is a part of machine learning that focuses on finding patterns and regularities in a given data set. Pattern recognition has its roots in engineering and is most often utilized in situations where there is an existing hypothesis or desired outcome, and the data must be mined in order to find patterns that support the existing theory. They are often marked by the "most likely" form of an output: looking for reasonable answers and outcomes from complex data sets based on grouping and patterns.

Pattern recognition algorithms have a distinct difference from pattern matching algorithms, which are based on exact matching of the pattern, rather than looking for grouped similarities. This means that pattern recognition is used for qualitative data, while pattern matching is often used for more quantitative data. Non-exact (but close) patterns are useful for pointing to trends, indications, and generalized possibilities, all things that would be missed if the criteria was an exact match. One example of pattern recognition is the algorithms used to separate out spam in an email account.

Deep Learning

Deep learning, which is also often called hierarchically structured learning, or deep structured learning, is the process of applying artificial neural networks (AI technology patterned after the biological neural networks in the human brain) to discover hidden layers of meaning. Primarily, it is based on a cascading process of information gathering through nonlinear layers, where each successive layer is added to information gathered from previous layers, allowing for complex nonlinear interpretation of data. The system is based on developing hierarchies in the information surveyed, or the ability to triage information to develop a language of importance.

This kind of system is often helpful when used in technology that tracks action like a human eye, or works off of other complex nonlinear reasoning responsive technology. Some common concepts in deep learning include the credit assignment path, or CAP, which tracks the chain of transformations or phenomenon from input to output, allowing for conclusions to be drawn from complex processes. Also prevalent is the term deep/shallow, which is a measuring device for the layers of nonlinear data present. The value of deep learning is in understanding that tangible output comes from the nuanced interaction of multiple layers of nonlinear data interacting with themselves, and understanding that the concept of hierarchy is critical: the high (more abstract) levels of learning come from mining lower (more concrete) levels of learning to draw conclusions that can be acted upon. This kind of learning is sometimes called "greedy" learning. In machine learning, it is a critical concept in allowing machines to improve on performance, to directly use the human concept of learning from your mistakes, or even more importantly, learning from somebody else's mistakes.

While working algorithms date back to the 1960s, deep learning is often credited to the work done by scientists in the early 2000s, and is often utilized in machines that need to be able to interact with variable human function: voice or handwriting recognition, tracking human movement, or analyzing via processes like the human eye.

Induction Logic Reasoning

Induction logic reasoning is a basic scheme that allows for logic-based interpretation of behavior by weighing data against positive and negative examples and background information in order to create a hypothesis about the data.

Induction logic reasoning is often utilized in natural language analysis and bioinformatics.

Neural networks

In the 1980s, most of the early work of machine learning was based on the concepts of neural networks. Scientists developed the idea of artificial neural networks, which are modeled off of biological neural networks (the brains of animals and humans). Biological neural networks work off of difference and accumulation: they store and compare experiences, starting to develop patterns and predict the future based on these experiences. These experiences compiled with the reward centers in the brain start to dictate behavior, as a biological neural network will start to understand that certain behaviors start to dictate certain responses from the environment that correlate with having certain needs met.

This is how a young human might learn that physically hitting people will drive them away, which leads to needs of food and warmth and safety being more difficult to achieve. In this same example, we can see the difference between how an artificial neural network and a biological neural network function morally and philosophically. If a robot learned through their artificial neural network not to hit people, it would be because of a clear accumulation of data that shows it does not serve the desired outcome. In the ways humans interpret and narrate our behaviors, the assumption of "morality" emerges:

most societies believe that there is something larger than cause and effect accumulation at play in our behavior choices. We don't hit each other not just because it gives us the desired biological need-based outcomes, but also because of larger ideas of "community" and "togetherness", abstractions that are difficult to translate into the language of programming artificial intelligence. Senses of "right" and "wrong" start to emerge inherently in the ways that humans self-referentially understand their biological response networks. This is at the core of a lot of critique and misunderstanding of artificial neural networks.

In the early days of machine learning, these systems were largely based on perception systems: the process of using specific criteria to separate and rank data based on the difference, or using binary classifiers in an algorithm to separate and classify things. However, as time went on, the tide turned in the world of AI, and machine learning became caught in the base criticisms of generalized linear models of statistics by those supporting logic based knowledge systems. In short, there were complex questions of where the data was coming from and how it was gathered and the inherent problems of objectivity in these data sets.

Expert Systems

By the mid-1980s, expert systems had taken popularity. These were systems based on what scientists thought mimicked the way humans made decisions: if-then propositions. There are two parts to expert systems: the knowledge base and the inference engine. The knowledge base is the pool of known facts and data. The inference engine applies the facts to the data in order to deduce new facts. Expert systems are often looked at as the first successful forms of artificial intelligence, as this ability to create new knowledge via deducing new facts from the knowledge base is a critical moment in artificial intelligence: the made creature is "thinking" on its own. Its programming allows for new growth, not just mimicry.

In the 1990s, machine learning became its own field. The focus became less about creating artificial intelligence as a means to its own end, and more about the practical applications of machine learning. This corresponded with the rise of the internet, and the incredible wealth of information that had the wide-reaching possibility for a field that relies on data, and lots of it.

Naive Bayes Systems

Obviously, when you are confronted with endless amounts of data, the processes by which you start looking at and studying this overwhelming quantity of data becomes of tantamount importance. One of the baseline computational practices for looking at data is the naive Bayes.

Naive Bayes is a term based off of Bayes's Theorem and has been used since the 1950s with data-retrieval systems. It's a way of separating out data into different categories, often used today in the process such as how to filter news into categories, or how your spam emails are separated out from your primary inbox, etc, using features such as word frequency. Today, we often see it used in systems that rely heavily on predictability in the outcome, such as automated medical diagnoses in the hospital and online technology.

The move from Bayes's theorem to naive Bayes is a crucial moment. There are now many variants of Bayesian systems, but at their core, they all have one thing in common: there is a basic assumption that Bayesian systems do not consider any factor to be dependant on others, allowing data sets to be endlessly variable, and (at least in theory) cutting down on subjective bias in outcome.

In the early 2000s, the Bayesian model was largely surpassed by decision trees and random forests as the primary useful model, but machine learning owes a lot of its early progress to naive Bayes models. Despite the fact that far-reaching independence assumptions about a set of data or variables are often inaccurate (especially when factors of human behavior and sociology are considered) the naive Bayes model has a lot to teach us, and has proven to be incredibly useful in alleviating the problems that researchers and programmers often find in what's referred to as the "curse of dimensionality" a phenomenon that results in huge data fields, where the interplay between data leads to the inability to use the data effectively.

Unsupervised and supervised learning algorithms

One of the critical pieces of understanding how machine learning works are understanding supervised and unsupervised learning algorithms. At its core, it's a simple concept: in supervised learning, the machine is trained using output data sets. In an unsupervised learning algorithm, there are no output data sets, with the information separated into different classes. Perhaps the most simple way of saying this is that supervised learning algorithms provide a correct resulting answer, while unsupervised learning algorithms are not. Supervised learning algorithms are self-referential; they know what their desired outcome is from the get-go. They use data sets, usually involving an input object, and the desired output value. In many situations where artificial intelligence is being utilized, this is actually ideal: when humans use machines, it's most often because we want a specific and desired outcome, and we want it to happen consistently. We want our toast toasted to the setting we put it on. Every time. We don't want the machine to get confused, or to have too many options to weigh. This example (although running the risk of being incredibly oversimplified) illustrates the power of a supervised learning algorithm.

That being said, we can see how human behavior doesn't follow this kind of trajectory. Humans operate largely out of patterns, it's true- perhaps (sticking with the same example) we have toast in the morning for breakfast. Once we decide to make the toast, perhaps we do have almost machine-esque desires for consistency. But, if we allow the system itself to expand, a huge amount of difficult to account for data points enter the set. What if the machine was responsible for deciding what you were going to eat for breakfast, rather than just responding to the desire to toast bread? In this system, we clearly see the need for an unsupervised learning algorithm.

What are the factors that play into what you decide to eat in the morning? Did you eat a big dinner? Are you planning on exercising after breakfast? Did you stay up late last night? Are you, in general, a breakfast eater? How hot is it? Do you want something hot or cold? As you can see, factors of the past, predictions, and knowledge of the future, and a wide variety of environmental factors are all at play. This is where unsupervised learning algorithms are helpful: there is no single outcome that satisfies everybody. Instead, there is a need to synthesize wide-reaching data and funnel those into some kind of sense-making filter that allows for cohesive sensation.

And, there's that odd human factor that a machine never experiences organically: boredom. If a human succeeds in typical patterning, eventually a dissatisfaction might grow entirely because of their success in patterning, and they will require a break purely for the novelty of something new, of an outlier in the system. As we start asking for machines to take on the work of human decision making, new systems of interpreting data become more and more necessary. More and more, we aren't asking machines to provide simple and clear one-outcome solutions to problems, but instead, we are asking machines to take up the job of helping us interpret our

48

environments, our pasts, and our predictions for the future, and offer us possible solutions to the interplay between these factors. A perfect example of this is the algorithms used for shopping on the internet-Facebook is constantly mining for what you search for elsewhere on the internet, and combining it with factors such as your combined demographic information on your profile, and factors such as the season, and letting those influence the flow of ads on your site. The results of this are surprisingly effective: a sixteen-year-old woman with a Facebook account who spent time searching for dresses on the internet and mentions "high school" in several posts is guaranteed to get a lot of pop up ads for dresses when prom season comes around. And the odds are, she's looking for a prom dress.

Decision Trees

Decision trees are a predictive modeling approach used in data mining, statistics, and most importantly for our purposes, machine learning. The model involves using observational data (often described as the branches of the trees) to make conclusions or classifications of some sort, which is illustrated visually by the leaves of the trees. There are two kinds of decision tree modeling systems: when a discrete conclusion can be reached (often represented by real numbers) then it's called a classification tree. If discrete conclusions can't be reached, and the target variable takes continuous form, it's called a regression tree.

The advantages to a decision tree model are numerous: first, it is often cited as operating much the way a human brain works, so it creates systems that sync well with how we view the world and operate in it. They operate well with qualitative data, unlike other models that require normalization of the data prior to input, as well as being able to handle large amounts of data, and can function to analyze both qualitative and quantitative data. On the other hand, they are often criticized as being overly complex (an inherent problem in a system that can use both qualitative and quantitative modeling), which is often referred to as "over lifting" the data set. To deal with this complexity, some researchers and programmers prefer the "decision stump", which is a single input modeling system where the decision stump connects directly to the "leaves", allowing less variance and complex interpretation of the data, but yielding clearer results. Decision tree modeling is a system used quite often by data mining companies, as well as a fundamental piece of machine learning.

Random Decision Forests

Random forests are a unit of research that corrects the problem of overlifting that occurs in utilizing decision trees. Creating a random forest involves utilizing a grouping of decision trees during training time, then using the mode or the mean of said forest to create a data set that corrects the problem of overlifting in an individual data summation from a decision tree. What makes decision trees so popular and successful is also their downfall: they often have low bias and incredibly high variance in the predictability of outcome, making them human-like in many ways (thus, their success) and also almost impossible to apply practically. The solution is to group large amounts of trees together, create a forest, and then mine the entire set with a particular set of sub-criteria, allowing for the averaged results of a large amount of complex data, giving a simple enough result that it can be practically allowed. This is called a "bagging algorithm". In addition, there is what's called a "neighborhood" element, where the results from a bagging algorithm are compared to results from the data from the forest that surrounds the original forests, allowing for comparative data, which can often result in accurate predictions about the entire data set as well as the future characteristics of evolving data.

The Moral and Philosophical Implications of Machine Learning

We often see examples of machine learning (and the potential benefits and consequences) in popular media and science fiction. There are countless movies and books that address the possibility of machine learning gone amok; robots, computers, or some other form of AI's are programmed to respond and change to their own experiences and/or a changing environment. At some point in the plot of these books and movies, there is the inevitable switch where we realize that there is still a missing element in AI: morality, the ability to love, etc- all the qualities that we like to hold dear as being essentially "human", and unable to be replicated by a machine. This narrative points to a deep cultural fear: what does it mean when machines start to look and respond more and more like humans?

Some of these questions are addressed within the world of machine learning, and some of them seem to require conversation and consideration from the larger worlds of philosophy and cultural critique. Within the world of machine learning, questions of morality seem to be centered around the fields of roboethics and machine ethics- machine ethics concerned with the ethic imprinted in or propagated by the actions of the machines, and roboethics primarily being concerned with the implications of the actions of an AI in the larger world. Often, this conversation is consumed by questions about the possibility of an AI to "feel" and "think" ethically. While this is an enticing question worthy of delving deeply, there is an entire another complex side to the issue. We don't often think of the moral and legal ramifications of an AI. For example, let's say that self-driving cars are responsible for 50% fewer deaths than human drivers. In the deaths that still occur, who is responsible, and in what way? Is nobody responsible? Is it the programmer? Is it the individual unit, which at this point in the imaginary example would probably have the technology in place to "think"? And what does it mean to hold a machine responsible? Is it taken apart or locked away, deemed somehow morally reprehensible for its actions the way a human would be? Or is that a value that we cannot directly translate from the human world to the world of machines?

In thinking about morality and an AI, there are two terms that are often cited; autonomy and ethical sensitivity. Autonomy refers to what the machine is capable of, and ethical sensitivity refers to what the machine is able to understand the implications of its actions. In most situations with artificial intelligence today, the programmers of said AI is able to account for most moral situations and dictate the response to fall on the side of commonly held human morals. For example, if there was an AI in charge of partial caretaking for elderly patients in a nursing home, a programmer could look at the situation, and anticipate quite a few problems that have moral implications. Let's say that one of the scenarios would be that an elderly patient might resist taking their medication, due to depreciating metal capacity from dementia. This is a moral situation that is likely to occur. The programmers would be able to teach the machine how to deal with this and give it a few possible (morally approved) actions based on a variety of specific inputs from the scenario weighed against laws, what the specific patient needs for their health and well-being, etc. This is a readily-anticipated moral situation, and the scientists could rig the results, as it were, by dictating the desired outcome. This is referred to a "top down" scenario in machine learning. But the very basic nature of machine learning in AI's insinuate a world where this will quickly not become feasible. Machine learning is pushing us toward the world where more and more machines are able to learn and respond autonomously to situations that do not have a prescribed outcome. This kind of top down machine learning with AI has the downside of being narrow and overly prescriptive: it doesn't allow for machines to understand how to respond to situations that do not match exact input criteria, leaving them unable to respond appropriately to situations with variable input or complex features.

What's referred to as the "bottom up" scenario in machine learning is much more similar to the way that humans learn morality: by witnessing their own behavior in contrast to the rest of their given society, and adjusting and learning by doing this.

In many ways, the question of morality in machines requires something that is almost impossible for humans to do: to define and understand their own specific moral mode, make it universal, and then be able to put it into programmable and machine learnable terms. For an example, let's say that it was agreed that an AI should exhibit utilitarianism. At its most basic definition, this seems to be a computational concept: actions should be chosen that allow for the highest expression of utility. But this inherently starts to unravel itself: how far into the future does the action need to resonate? Is it short term utility, or utility that has the most longevity? What are the specific criteria that an AI could use to measure utility? These questions are incredibly complex.

In scenarios such as this, it becomes very clear that in order for us to ever develop rules or procedure for installing artificial intelligence with a moral code, it would be necessary to develop it for ourselves, in specific terms of action, time, place, and procedure. While morality feels obvious in many ways, it is a specific and complex problem, and the decision for how to instill this in AI is not just a questions for programmers, but for all of us. It seems that there is a lot of value in using an interdisciplinary approach to this conversation, pulling from the work done in philosophy and even science fiction. The short fiction author Issac Asimov came up with a set of rules for his AI creations: First, do not harm humans. Second, obey humans. Third, protect its own existence.

Dishearteningly enough, the majority of his work is devoted to how these rules (which seem, at least on the surface, a great starting place for instilling morality) can be horribly misconstrued, leading to pain and suffering.

The moral of the story here is perhaps that most ideas of human morality are not based on logic and clear linear reasoning, and they require a nuanced and skilled interpretation of a hugely wide and deep understanding of many things simultaneously: current physical environment, the past and future of the individual, as well as the larger social community and context, and the past and futures of those elements, as well as the conceptual framework and historical and social significance of all of these things. Those are incredibly difficult to break down into computable data. It doesn't feel as though machine learning has yet achieved this ability, but with the increasing aptitude of replicating models of learning based on the human brain, it is possible that this is not far off.

ISBN-13: 978-1718911147

ISBN-10: 1718911149